Laxity, Moderation and Extremism in Islam

Aisha B. Lemu

INTERNATIONAL INSTITUTE OF ISLAMIC THOUGHT
Herndon, Virginia
London

Published 1993 by IIIT—
International Institute of Islamic Thought
Headquarters:
555 Grove Street
Herndon, VA. 22070, USA

London Office:
P.O. Box 126
Richmond, Surrey, TW9 2UD, UK

British Library Cataloguing in Publication Data
Lemu, B. Aisha
Laxity, Moderation and Extremism in Islam
I. Title II. Al Shaikh-Ali, Anas
305.6
ISBN 0-912463-95-3

Occasional Papers Series' Editors

Dr A S al Shaikh-Ali
Dr Riyadh A. Nourallah
Rashid Messaoudi

Design by Zafar 'Abbas Malik

Printed in the USA by
International Graphics
4411 41st Street
Brentwood, Maryland, 20722

CONTENTS

The *Occasional Papers* Series v

Introduction 1

Definition 1

Manifestations of Extremism 9

Causes of Extremism 11

The Remedies for Extremism 15

Thoughtfulness: A Basic Value 19

Allah's Sunan 24

Honoring and Respecting True Scholarship 25

Da'wah: A Question of Tact and Wisdom 26

Idealism, Daydreams and the Immediate Task 27

Belief in Human Goodness 28

Extremism: An Impediment to *Da'wah* 29

Status of Western Languages 34

Correcting Evil-Doing 36

Publications of the IIIT 42

THE *OCCASIONAL PAPERS* SERIES

The publication program of the International Institute of Islamic Thought (IIIT) has already addressed important issues in the field of Islamic thought and the Islamization of knowledge. In this respect a number of books have already appeared in several languages under thirteen main series: *Accessing the Islamic Intellectual Heritage; Dissertations*; *Human Development*; *Indices; Islamic Methodology*; *Islamization of Culture*; *Islamization of Knowledge*; *Issues in Islamic Thought*; *Lectures*; *Occasional Papers*; *Perspectives on Islamic Thought*; *Research Monographs* and *Studies in the Islamization of Knowledge*.

The *Occasional Papers* series, published by the Institute's London Office, covers a number of research papers, articles and lectures from the Institute's world-wide program as well as from Muslim scholars willing to make contributions. These are presented individually in the form of booklets that can be easily read or referred to. It is hoped that the booklets will reach students, scholars, and specialists as well as major sections of the world's Muslims alike in order to generate a fruitful debate on the vital issue of Islamization, and to create an awareness of the intellectual crisis in its various shapes and forms, while encouraging an active role in the proposed course of action and solution. This series is also translated into other languages.

Much of this paper is a summary of Shaikh Yusuf al Qaradawi's *Islamic Awakening between Rejection and Extremism*. The paper has effectively covered the topic and brought to light many useful references from the Qur'an, the Hadith and various historical sources.

The use of Islamic terminology in transliteration is a policy of the IIIT. Some of the terms used are untranslatable, while others are so important that the Institute felt that familiarity with them is necessary for a better understanding of Islamic issues. These terms have been footnoted once or sometimes explained briefly between brackets. All those which have not yet been accepted in Anglo-Saxon dictionaries are in italic. As many of these occur more than once, readers are advised to refer to the relevant footnotes whenever necessary.

When mentioning dates the Islamic one comes first separated from the Gregorian one by a slash. When an Islamic date is mentioned alone, it is followed by AH.

The translation of the Qur'an used in this series is that of Yusuf Ali (Amana Corporation, revised, 1989). However we made changes to verses quoted from it whenever we deemed it necessary for the sake of elucidation and precision of meaning.

IIIT, London
1413/1993

Introduction

This is a very important issue for us to address in the Muslim world today. Paradoxically, though, it is an issue we seldom address. Why is it so important, and why do we seldom address it? It is important because it affects our relationship with one another as well as with non-Muslims, and thus the spread of Islam—all crucial concerns for the future of the Ummah. Why then do we seldom speak about it? Because to do so is to run the risk of being abused, misunderstood and quoted out of context by people who cannot tolerate any opinion other than their own, even if that other opinion has a sound basis in Islamic teachings.

For much of what follows I am deeply indebted to the celebrated scholar and writer Shaikh Yusuf al Qaradawi, most particularly in his *Islamic Awakening between Rejection and Extremism*[1]. This book has effectively covered the topic and brought to light many useful references from the Qur'an, the Hadith and other historical sources. A lot of my paper is summary and quotation from al Qaradawi's book. However, I have endeavored to bring to the topic some insights gained from my experience in Nigeria and other Muslim countries, though I have no intention to relate my argument consistently to any specific locality or group. Rather, I hope to make my observations general enough to be pertinent to as wide a context as possible, while recognizing the need to address individual communities with individual prognoses and insights.

Definition

For a start, it is essential to define the terms used in the title of this paper: Laxity, Moderation and Extremism. The definition of **laxity** is easy. It means carelessness and looseness. Laxity in Islam means failure to follow the basic teachings—negligence of

---

1. New edition revised and edited by A.S. al Shaikh-Ali and Mohammad B.E. Wasfy, jointly published by IIIT and American Trust Publications, Herndon, Va. 1991. Hereafter cited as *IA*.

the prescribed acts of worship and failure to submit to the moral guidance of the Shari'ah in respect of various aspects of the Islamic way of life. This may be due to ignorance, weakness, upbringing, social pressure, hostile educational and cultural policy, or lack of understanding of the moral principles and the wisdom underlying Islamic injunctions and prohibitions. Laxity refers not to those who have consciously rejected Islam. Rather, it refers to those who believe in God but do not avail themselves of His guidance. This condition can therefore often be cured by tactful *da'wah*[2] and reasoned discussion whereby the careless person learns to care about his or her relationship with God and with other people.

What then is **moderation** in Islam? Moderation means to carry out to the best of one's ability what Allah (SWT)[3] has prescribed and to avoid what He has forbidden, to understand the wisdom of His Laws and moral guidance and to grasp and apply the basic Islamic principles to every new situation as it arises. Having complied with the prescribed aspects of worship and moral discipline, a moderate person may, if he is so inclined, attempt to purify himself and come closer to Allah by supererogatory acts of worship in the form of voluntary *salāh*[4], *sawm*[5], *zakāh*[6], hajj[7],

2. *da'wah*: Invitation; call. Refers to the duty on Muslims to invite or call upon others to return to the straight and natural path of Islam. This, according to the Qur'an, has to be done with wisdom and gracious advice. *Da'wah* is addressed to both Muslims and non-Muslims.
3. SWT—*Subhānahu wa Ta'ālā*: May He be praised and may His transcendence be affirmed. Said when using the name of the divine majesty.
4. *salāh* (pl. *salawāt*): The supreme act of worship in Islam, inadequately translated as 'prayer'. Basically there are five appointed ritual *salawāt*; but a person can—and does—perform voluntary ones.
5. *sawm*: Abstaining from any eating, drinking, smoking or sexual activity from dawn to sunset, every day of the month of Ramadan. Fasting—as cited above—can also be voluntary.
6. *zakāh*: The obligatory sharing of wealth with the poor and the community at the yearly rate of 2.5% of appropriated wealth above a certain minimum. It also refers to general charity that is strongly encouraged by divine injunctions.

'umrah[8], *dhikr*[9] and loving conduct towards other people. The way and the degree to which such a person does these depend on a number of things including one's natural temperament, understanding and level of *imān*[10]. Moderation therefore covers a wide range of spiritual states.

According to a number of *aḥādīth*[11], the Prophet (ṢAAS)[12] praised those who adopted a moderate approach to worship. Worship, he said, should be done with freshness of heart, not as an exhausting routine carried on in spite of fatigue. Therefore various provisions were made in the Qur'an and the Hadith to ease things—for travellers, for the sick, for pregnant or nursing women, for the old, for the poor, because "On no soul does Allah place a burden greater than it can bear". (Qur'an 2:286)

The word **moderate** is sometimes taken to mean 'only half-committed'. This is a mistake. A moderate may be just as deeply committed as an extremist, but they differ in the way they fulfil their commitment. Moderation is therefore not a matter of commitment to Islam or lack of it, but of how to practice Islam, how to interpret and apply its teachings, how to relate to other people and how to go about calling other people to the truth.

If I look back to the first decade that I spent in Nigeria, from 1966 to 1976, I was struck by the high level of tolerance on the

---

7. ḥajj: The fifth pillar of Islam consisting of acts performed at Makkah on the ninth and tenth days of Dhū al Ḥijjah, the last month of the Islamic lunar year.
8. *'umrah*: A minor pilgrimage to Makkah, which does not count towards fulfillment of the hajj, may be made at any time.
9. *dhikr*: The remembrance of Allah (SWT), or His presence in the consciousness of mankind.
10 *imān:* The conviction or certainty, that Allah is indeed the one and only God and that Muhammad is His last prophet.
11 hadith (Pl. *aḥādīth*): The verbalized form of a tradition of the Prophet Muhammad (ṢAAS) constitutive of his Sunnah.
12 SAAS—*Salla Allāhu 'Alayhi was Sallam*: May the peace and blessings of Allah be upon him; said whenever the name of the Prophet Muhammad is mentioned, or whenever he is referred to as the Prophet of Allah.

part of the Muslims—a tolerance that seemed sometimes to stem from a simple and trusting nature. Students in schools were still generally being taught their religion by traditional Mallams. Islam meant how to perform prayers, the rules of fasting, memorization of the Qur'an and so on. Christians were a minority who posed little threat and they enjoyed much tolerance from the Muslims. Within a decade the situation began to change. Students now began to get their knowledge of Islam from a variety of sources: young trained teachers, a variety of books in English, and a great number of magazines and newspaper articles. They also began to follow Islamic programmes on the radio and television, some of which were well-informed, some not. In addition they learned from lectures and camps organized by Islamic groups and organizations, who would invite anyone with Islamic interest to give lectures. Many young students themselves gave lectures and conducted group studies of the Qur'an and Hadith. This has continued to be the common pattern of learning to this day. It is the age of the amateur in Islamic Studies and anyone can stand up and have a go, even those with very limited knowledge. Obviously this is the result, in many Muslim countries, of the imposed secularization of education by an elite dedicated to promoting ideas and theories incompatible with the Islamic worldview.

The outcome of this has its good and its bad side. On the good side, young Muslims have come to realize that Islam is not just prayers, fasting and memorization of the Qur'an. They have a much broader idea of the implications of Islam as a way of life, together with its social, economic and political teachings. The interest generated by these discoveries has brought about a re-awakening among young Muslims, and many of them, with the enthusiasm and the dedication of youth, have identified themselves with the Islamic cause and tried to conduct their lives on Islamic principles. Many naturally aspire for an Islamic form of government based on the Shari'āh[13] as existed before the colonial era. At the same time they have become much more aware of the

---

13 Shari'āh: The collective name for all the laws of Islam, including Islam's whole religious and liturgical, ethical and jurisprudential systems.

political, cultural and even religious efforts by foreign powers to undermine Islam and the Shari'āh.

But the re-awakening also has its dangerous side. Students have become confused and often divided through being exposed to such a variety of information and views from so many different sources. Young Muslims with poor standards of general education and no firm grounding in Islam can hardly be expected to possess a clear judgement with which to assess what they read or are told about Islam. Consequently they can be easily led, by those who pose to have knowledge, to take up positions of extremism and intolerance towards fellow Muslims who might not conform to their newly-acquired concept of Islam. Those Muslims who do not hold the same idea or possess the same fervour could be regarded as 'modern Muslims', hypocrites or even unbelievers, instead of brothers and sisters sharing the same faith.

And who could blame the youth for dividing themselves and taking extreme positions when they could see some of their elders doing the same thing over other issues.

What then is meant by **extremism**? It is important to be clear about the definition because the word is often used improperly to describe anyone who is committed to following the basic and well-known teachings of Islam. Al Qaradawi writes:

> Literally, extremism means being situated at the farthest possible point form the centre. Figuratively, it indicates a similar remoteness in religion and thought, as well as behavior. One of the main consequences of extremism is exposure to danger and insecurity. Islam therefore recommends moderation and balance in everything: in belief, *'ibādah*, conduct and legislation. This is the straightforward path that Allah (SWT) calls *al ṣirāt al mustaqīm*; one distinct from all others which are followed by those who earn Allah's anger and those who go astray. Moderation, or balance, is not only a general characteristic of Islam, it is a fundamental landmark. The Qur'an says: "Thus have we made of you an

> Ummah justly balanced." (Qur'an 2:143)[14]

Islamic texts call upon Muslims to exercise moderation and to reject and oppose all kinds of extremism: *ghuluw* (excessiveness) and *tashdīd* (bigotry). For example, the Prophet is reported to have said:

> Beware of excessiveness in religion. [People] before you have perished as a result of [such] excessiveness.[15]

In other words excess may eventually develop into a larger problem and even become a threat to the well-being and security of the Ummah—indeed, in the same way as laxity can do.

According to another hadith, the Prophet said: "Ruined were those who indulged in hair-splitting"[16], and he repeated it three times. Imam Al Nawawi commented that this referred to those who were excessive in utterance and action, resulting in loss in this life and the Hereafter.

According to other *aḥādīth*, the Prophet said:

> Verily this religion is easy, and none shall be severe in religion but it will overcome him: he shall turn it into a stone and make it a tomb.[17]

> Do not overburden yourselves, lest you perish. People [before you] overburdened themselves and perished. Their remains are found in hermitages and monasteries.[18]

The Prophet always resisted any tendency towards religious excess, even in *'ibādah*[19]. Numerous *aḥādīth* testify to this. Islam seeks to create a balance between the needs of the body and those of the soul, between this world and the hereafter, between

---

14 *IA*, p.21
15 Reported by Ahmad, Nasa'i and Ibn Majah.
16 Reported by Muslim.
17 Reported by Bukhari.
18 Reported by Muslim and Abu Dawud.
19 *'ibādah*: The act or action of serving God.

the right of man to live life to its full, and his duty to worship and obey his Creator.

The various forms of *'ibădah* in Islam purify the soul and establish harmony and brotherhood in the community, without hindering the building of culture and civilization. Muslims are to pray for "the good of this world and the good in the Hereafter." (Qur'an 2:201).

If Allah does not wish us to be extreme in our worship of Him—worship being the reason for our creation—there is no reason to believe that He wants us to be extreme in our conduct towards one another, or in other aspects of our life.

The Qur'an speaks of enjoyment of Life:

> O children of Adam! Wear your beautiful apparel at every time and place of prayer. Eat and drink, but waste not [by excess,] for Allah loves not those who waste. Say: who has forbidden the beautiful gifts of Allah which He has produced for His servants and the things clean and pure which He has provided for sustenance? (7:30-31)

In another verse it says:

> O you who believe! Make not unlawful the good things Allah has made lawful to you. But commit no excess, for Allah does not like those given to excess. Eat of the things which Allah has provided you, lawful and good, but fear Allah, in Whom you believe. (4:86-88)

The Sunnah[20] emphasizes that people should give due right to their Lord, to themselves, to their families and to other people. All these warnings are necessary because there is something inherently wrong with excessiveness and extremism. Firstly, it is too repulsive for ordinary human nature to endure or tolerate. The majority could never put up with excessiveness, even if a few

---

20 Sunnah: With capital S, it means the path and example of the Prophet, consisting of all that he said, did, approved of or condemned. See also footnote 36.

could do so for a short time. The Shari'āh addresses the whole of humanity, not just a special group who have a unique capacity for endurance. Once Mu'adh ibn Jabal led *ṣalāh* and prolonged it, and some people complained to the Prophet. The Prophet said to him: "O Mu'adh! Are you putting the people on trial?" and repeated it three times.[21]

On another occasion he spoke with anger to an Imam, saying:

> Some of you make people dislike to do good deeds [that is *ṣalāh*]. So whoever among you leads people in *ṣalāh* should shorten it because among them are the weak,the old and the one who has business to attend to.[22]

When the Prophet sent Mu'adh and Abu Musa al Ash'ari to Yemen, he gave them the following advice: "Facilitate [religious matters to people] and do not make [things] difficult. Obey each other and do not differ [among yourselves]."[23]

Secondly, excessiveness tends to be short-lived. Al Qaradawi says: "I have often met people who were known for their strictness and extremism; then I lost contact with them for a while. When I enquired about them after a period of time, I found out that they had either deviated or taken the opposite extreme, or at least lagged behind." [24] So the Prophet said:

> Do those deeds which you can do easily, as Allah will not get tired [of giving rewards] till you get bored and tired [of performing religious deeds]...and the most beloved deed to Allah is the one which is done regularly even if it were little.[25]

The third defect of excessiveness is that it is often at someone else's expense—that is, someone else is likely to suffer neglect or inconvenience as a result of the extremist's preoccupation with

---

21 Reported by Bukhari.
22 Reported by Bukhari.
23 Reported by Bukhari and Muslim.
24 *IA*, p.26.
25 Reported by Bukhari and Muslim.

doing more than others.

If extremism refers to whatever is furthest from the center or the middle course, and is condemned in the Qur'an and by the Prophet, it is important to distinguish where the middle course lies and where the extreme lies. People's perceptions of this are bound to differ. Obviously, personal piety, family background and the environment affect our perceptions of what is extreme, moderate or lax.

For example, people brought up in a strict Muslim environment tend to regard any deviation with horror and aversion. At the other extreme are some whose background is so un-Islamic that they regard even minimal adherence to Islam as a kind of extremism. They express surprise at someone who performs *ṣalāh* five times a day, cast doubt over what is clearly *ḥarām*[26], and even regard the wearing of *ḥijāb*[27] as an act of extremism, fanaticism and backwardness.

Manifestations of Extremism

The manifestations of what could clearly be identified as extremism are numerous. The following are among them:

1. **Bigotry:** The extremist believes that he is right and cannot be wrong. He regards anyone who differs from him as an enemy or at best an ignorant person. He cannot tolerate differences of opinion. Al Qaradawi remarks:

> The issue becomes even more critical when such a person develops a tendency to coerce others, not necessarily physically but by accusing them of *bid'ah*[28], laxity, *kufr*[29]

---

26 *ḥarām* (pl. *muḥarramāt*): That which Allah has explicitly forbidden humans to do and for which He specified a penalty.

27 *ḥijāb*: The Islamic style of dress for women.

28 *bid'ah*: Condemned innovation.

29 *kufr*: The act of declaring solemnly one's disbelief. See footnote 31.

and deviation. Such intellectual terrorism is as terrifying as physical terrorism.[30]

2. **Excessiveness in all things**: The extremist is committed to excessiveness and attempts to force others to do likewise, despite good reasons for Islam having made things easy. As the Qur'an says: "Allah intends every facility for you: He does not want to put you in difficulties." (2:185)

3. **Sternness without consideration of time or place**: Examples include causing difficulties for converts in non-Islamic societies and pursuing controversies over such matters as dress, sitting on the floor instead of on chairs, eating on the floor, eating without cutlery and so on, all the while insisting that everyone must comply with their wish. Ironically, those who initiate and sustain such bitter controversies over matters of detail are often neglectful of essential religious duties to their parents, wives, children and neighbours.

4. Linked to this is **ill-mannered treatment of people**, and **a crude approach to calling people to Islam**—which generally serves to frighten them away rather than draw them closer.

5. **Suspicion**: Contrary to the spirit and teachings of Islam which encourage Muslims to think well of others, the extremist is always ready to accuse people and jump to conclusions of guilt the moment he suspects a person of anything. If anyone tries to state a moderate and authentically Islamic position, the extremist accuses him of transgression, laxity, westernization, disrespect for the Sunnah, or even unbelief. Allah says:

> O you who believe! Avoid suspicion as much [as possible], for suspicion in some cases is a sin. (49:12).

---

30 *IA*, p.34.

Such suspicion is related to pride, the first act of disobedience of Satan who claimed: "I am better than he is." (38:76)

Causes of Extremism

Extremism does not originate by chance. It should be realized that such a complex phenomenon has numerous causes, both direct and indirect, some recent and some going far back in time.

1- The first cause of extremism is **lack of knowledge** of and insight into the underlying purposes, spirit and essence of faith. Some extremists who claim to be versed in Shar'iah lose sight of the underlying purpose and essence of Islam. They insist on total literal application of certain *aḥādīth* without consideration of the circumstances in the contemporary world under which they are applied.

Shaikh al Qaradawi gives several examples of this. One is the hadith in which the Prophet advised against carrying a copy of the Qur'an into the land of the *kuffār*[31]. If we look at the reason underlying this prohibition, we conclude that it was his concern that in the war-situation of the time, the *kuffār* might desecrate or harm the Qur'an if it fell into their hands. This is not normally the situation nowadays—Muslims travel all over the world carrying their Qur'an for personal reading without fear of desecration. Moreover, availability of the Qur'an in many languages is nowadays an important part of *da'wah* in many non-Muslim countries, and a cause of their people embracing Islam.

---

31 *kāfir* (pl. *kuffār* or *kāfirūn*): The person guilty of declaring solemnly his/her disbelief (*kufr*). To say solemnly that Allah is not God, or is not the subject of each of His attributes, or that Muhammad is not His Prophet, or that anything in the Qur'an is not verbatim truth or revelation from Allah. See footnote 29.

A second example is the hadith that a woman should not travel alone without a *maḥram*[32]. This practice serves a useful purpose, offering a woman physical protection and assistance on long, arduous or dangerous journeys, as well as protection from sexual harassment and moral danger, which under certain circumstances could befall a woman travelling alone[33]. However, there are circumstances when it is difficult or impossible for her to take a *maḥram* with her: modern circumstances of full-time employment, both for men and women, the decline of the extended family living close together, and the high cost of travel may make it impossible in some cases for a woman to travel with family escort. Moreover, some modern modes of travel carry no more danger, physical or moral, than any other human activity. A woman may be escorted to an airport, board a plane, and in a few hours cover thousands of miles and be met safely at the other end. If a *maḥram* were to require a return air ticket to escort her to her destination, and another return ticket for a second journey to escort her back, it would make the whole journey financially impossible for ordinary people. Or there may be no close relative free to escort her. Yet it may be an essential journey or a journey of great use or benefit, and the husband may be fully confident that it can be done without physical or moral danger. This is an area where judgement should surely be applied in order to facilitate things for people where necessary.

A third example is a hadith which forbids a Muslim husband, returning to his family after long absence, from coming home at night. There may be two reasons for this: firstly to avoid giving the impression he suspects his wife

---

32 *maḥram*: A male relative who, because of kinship ties, is not permitted to marry the woman in question.

33 Sexual harassment in the West has become so acute in the 1990's that it has led to some well-publicized trials and to an unprecedented tightening of legislation. Still, the problem endures—in the West and worldwide. (Eds.)

and is trying to catch her unawares; secondly, to give her time to prepare herself and the house to receive him. Nowadays a telephone call, letter or telegram can inform a wife of her husband's expected time of arrival. Moreover modern modes of travel often necessitate arrival by night, and few people would insist a husband should go and stay in a nearby hotel for a night in order to comply with the hadith and arrive by daylight. The hadith at that time was meant to solve a problem. If applied nowadays, it could often create a problem where none exists. Yet there are some people who fail to grasp the underlying motive of such hadith. As al Qaradawi remarks: "This intellectual shallowness and lack of religious insight also manifest themselves in an intense interest in marginal issues at the expense of major ones."[34] Thus much time is spent debating issues such as beards, turbans, length of dress, photographs, and other minor optional details of worship, while compiling long lists of extra excessive prohibitions bent on making life intolerable.

Another aspect of this shallowness of knowledge is the inability to distinguish between major and minor degrees of *kufr*, *shirk*[35] or hypocrisy without any consideration to a person's inner motives, and wrong interpretation of allegorical texts of the Qur'an and the hadith.

Most of these problems of young extremists arise because such youths have not been taught by reliable ulama. They have received knowledge of sorts from books and newspapers, preachers and so called 'activists' who were themselves in some cases not properly taught.

2. A second cause of extremism is **lack of insight** into

---

34 *IA*, p.56.

35 *shirk*: Association of other beings with Allah; opposite of *tawḥīd*. *Mushrik* (pl. *mushrikūn*): The person who practices or believes in *shirk*.

reality and history as well as Allah's *sunnah*[36] or way of dealing with them in His creation. This causes the extremists to demand the impossible. They want to change the whole fabric of society—its thoughts, traditions, ethics, social, political and economic system by means unrelated to reality. They may show great courage and disregard for personal consequences, but without insight into the nature of reality their sacrifices are doomed to fail. The concept of a 'step-by-step' approach, which was adopted by the Prophet in Makkah has no appeal to the extremist. By contrast the latter wants immediate and complete transformation, and has no time for allowing long-term strategies to mature. In the absence of support from the majority of Muslims, he may resort to force or precipitate a crisis even though it may cause a setback to the long-term cause of Islam.

3. A third cause of extremism is its opposite—**laxity**, indifference to Islamic values and corruption as seen in societies around us—particularly when those in authority encourage it or at least fail to take the obvious and necessary steps to control it for the general good of society.

   The laws of the land are not necessarily based on the Shari'āh, the gap grows between rich and poor, and social injustice becomes more and more evident. Young Muslims witness these things and feel powerless. They are not in a position to "change things with their hands" as they have no authority to do so. They lack experience to know how to go about "changing things with their tongues"[37] so they bottle up their frustrations in their hearts until sometimes it boils over. For this some are duly punished, resulting in further frustration.

---

36 *sunnah* (pl.*sunan*):The pattern of Allah in ordering creation or any part or aspect of it usually referred to as 'cosmic laws'. See footnote 20.

37 The two quotations in this paragraph pertain to the hadith referred to in footnote 61.

Likewise on the international scene these people feel powerless in the face of suppression of Muslims in many parts of the world. They see many Muslim rulers apparently reduced to puppets in the hands of foreign powers. This generates a feeling of resentment of all non-Muslim foreigners and a suspicion of everything foreign, including modern knowledge—irrespective of the guilt or otherwise of the foreigners concerned or the usefulness of the knowledge to Muslims. They are labelled as *kuffār* and all their works as *kufr*.

4. Needless to say, extremism is often fanned by **political oppression**, practiced by rulers or regimes bent on imposing alien ideologies on Muslim societies and undermining the very teachings and worldview of Islam through various means, most particularly through the educational system. Such rulers are generally shored up by outside and self-seeking powers; and their continued suppression of Islamic feelings never fails to generate bitterness against and mistrust of everything foreign together with an advocacy of extremist attitudes, including outright violence. This vicious circle has wreaked incalculable damage on numerous Muslim countries to date.

The Remedies for Extremism

Having identified some of the symptoms and diagnosed some of the causes of extremism, what of the remedies?

The first step for a predominantly Muslim community must be to acknowledge and confirm its genuine commitment to Islam—not through slogans or constitutional clauses but by practical adherence to Islamic principles in the conduct of public affairs. This must be done with full commitment both to Islam and to the religious rights of non-Muslim minorities. This type of commitment to Islamic values by the governments of the Muslim world would certainly win a response from the general public, channel youthful idealism into useful directions, solve most of the internal problems and thus bring about greater stability. It is necessary, therefore, to conduct well-reasoned *da'wah* among people in government and administration.

Secondly, older people should show a greater understanding towards our youth, and have frequent and open discussions with them. They need patient treatment on an intellectual level. You cannot fight obstinacy or bigotry with another bigotry. Nor should we condemn religious extremism and yet keep silent about religious laxity. Freedom of expression must be defended and rational discussion used to bring order and sense to confused minds.

Thirdly, steps must be taken to increase the young people's indepth understanding of how to interpret the Qur'an and the Hadith so as to achieve a true insight into the Shari'āh.

Those who have this knowledge and insight must make it a duty to teach young Muslims on a regular basis, otherwise they will fall into the hands of half-baked shaikhs of shallow knowledge and little insight. Islamic organizations should give much attention to the training of young people.

The young need to know that:

1. A verse of the Qur'an or a hadith cannot be taken in isolation as an authority without reference to other verses and other *aḥādīth* that may elaborate, explain and qualify it. This is a field requiring expert knowledge.

2. It is necessary to distinguish between the eternal and unalterable principles of Islam and other teachings which are directed to particular needs.

3. It is necessary to take into account the diversity of our society. Social change and technological development have increased the admixture of people from many different backgrounds, between different nations and

different communities within nations. This applies not only to the mixture of Muslims and non-Muslims who must learn to live together, but even to Muslims and other Muslims. In many Muslim countries what is Islamically acceptable in one area may be regarded as very un-Islamic in another. Even the children of one family may have been brought up with stricter Islamic standards than others. We must learn to live with variety.

Our community, therefore, includes the strong and the weak, the learned and the ignorant, the highly-motivated and the poorly motivated, male and female, old and young—and they cannot all achieve the same standards in their understanding of and commitment to the application of Islam. This diversity should be taken into account in our attempts to guide others, or when giving *fatāwā*[38]. What we may find easy might be unbearably hard for some others. Therefore even an Islamic administration would not be advised to impose extreme standards on all.

As al Qaradawi says:

> A Muslim who seeks Allah's pleasure can choose to place restrictions on himself and stick to the most extreme and cautious opinions in his endeavor. He can deprive himself of all the means of entertainment such as singing, music, photography, television etc. But can any modern state afford to do without these? Can any effective journalism do without photography? Can any ministry of interior, a... passport office, immigration or traffic department or an educational institution do without photography which has become the most important means of discovering and preventing crimes and forgery? Can science or medicine be taught or practiced without pictures and photography? And what of satellite pictures for defence and weather forecasting? Can any contemporary state ignore the times it exists in and deprive its subjects of the incredible services of television relying only on the radio, on the grounds that television depends upon

---

38 *fatāwā* (sing. fatwah): A juristic opinion given by a *'ālim, mufti,* or *mujtahid* on any matter pertinent to Islamic law.

> photography which is *ḥarām* as some students of religious education argue these days? In short, a person's restrictions on himself can be tolerated and accepted, but it would be intolerable and unacceptable to force them on the various groups in the community as a whole. The Prophet Himself (ṢAAS) emphasized making things easy for the sake of the weaker members of the Ummah, as when he ordered those leading prayer to "shorten it for the sake of the old, the weak and those who have business to attend to."[39]

Differences of opinion were recognized as blessings by the early Muslims and the great scholars of old. They held varied opinions on many issues and did not make this a cause of ill-feeling and disunity between them. Such differences of opinion always existed and always will exist as they are a natural part of man's God-given nature. Any attempt to eradicate them will therefore fail and cause more harm than good. Rather we must learn *adab al ikhtilāf* (the ethics of disagreement)[40] as inherited from our early ulama[41].

Shaikh al Qaradawi comments:

> In this respect, I feel inclined to admit that the only religious leader who, in this age, has understood the essence and ethics of disagreement, was Hassan al Banna (d.1949). He brought up his followers to believe in and adhere to these ethics. Despite his unflinching commitment to the cause of Muslim solidarity and his sincere efforts to unite the various Muslim groups and make them agree at least on minimum Islamic concepts and principles, as is clear from his own work *al Uṣūl al 'Ishrūn*, he was convinced of the inevitability of disagreement on the subsidiary issues and the practical *aḥkām* of Islam. This he has eloquently discussed in many of his messages which have proved to be useful. In *Da'watunā* (Our *Da'wah*), al Banna spoke of the characteristics of his *da'wah* as being general ones which neither patronize a particular sect nor advocate a particular line of thought. Interest is in the core of the *dīn* and its essence; it hopes that all endeavors are

39 *IA*, p.116.

40 See Dr. Ṭāhā Jābir al 'Alwānī's *The Ethics of Disagreement in Islam*, IIIT, Herndon, Va. 1993.

41 *'ālim* (pl. ulama): Islamic scholar.

> united so that a more fruitful work can be done to produce greater results; it supports truth everywhere; it likes consensus and dislikes eccentricity; it attributes a great deal of the mishaps which have befallen Muslims to misguided disagreement and to disunity; it believes that love and unity are the two major factors of their victories, and that the only hope for invigorating and revitalizing the present-day Ummah lies in reviving and adopting the practices of the early generations of Muslims.[42]

He cites an occasion when Hassan al Banna was invited to give a lecture in a certain Egyptian village where the people were divided to the point of violence into two groups over whether *ṣalāt al tarāwīḥ*[43] should be twenty or eight *raka'āt*[44]—each basing their stand on accepted traditions.

> The way he handled this event is instructive to all of us. He first asked: "What is the juristic status of *ṣalāt al tarāwīḥ*?" The answer was: "A sunnah, and those who perform it are rewarded, those who do not are not punished." He then asked: "And what is the juristic status of brotherhood among Muslims?" The people replied: "*farḍ* [Obligatory], and it is one of the fundamentals of *īmān*". He then concluded: "Is it therefore logical or permissible according to Shari'āh to abandon a *farḍ* for a sunnah?" He then told them that if they preserved their brotherhood and unity and each went home and performed *ṣalāt al tarāwīḥ* according to his own genuine conviction, it would be far better than ...quarrelling.[45]

Thoughtfulness: A Basic Value

The Qur'an and the Hadith have made it clear that not all acts have the same value. Not all good acts are equally good, and not all bad acts are equally bad. Moreover the circumstances under

---

42 *IA*, p.121.

43 *ṣalāt al tarāwīḥ*: (Literally 'the prayer of pauses'). Extra prayers undertaken on a voluntary basis during the nights of the month of fasting, Ramadan. The prayer can comprise as much as forty *raka'āt*, with a pause after every four.

44 *rak'ah* (pl. *raka'āt*): Literally, 'bowing'. The *rak'ah* is a 'unit of prayer'. The number of *raka'āt* performed varies from one *ṣalah* to another.

45 *IA*, p.124.

which they are done could affect their praiseworthiness or blameworthiness.

It is wrong to pursue people's minor sins while ignoring major ones which compromise the essential character of Islam as a pure monotheistic religion. Such practices as witchcraft and fortune-telling, which are still rampant in our society often in Islamic disguise, are far more worthy of struggling against than differences in matters of personal choice or ordinary human weakness.

As we have pointed out, people are all different in respect of their knowledge, endurance and *imān*, and we have no right to dismiss the weak as if they were outside the fold of Islam.

The Qur'an specifically mentions this:

> Then We have given the book for inheritance to such of our servants as We have chosen: but there are among them some who wrong their own souls; some who follow a middle course; and some who are, by Allah's leave, foremost in good deeds. That is the highest grace. (35:32)

Shaikh al Qaradawi points out in this respect:

> All these types of people, including the person who wrongs himself, are included in the fold of Islam and belong to the chosen Islamic Ummah to whom Allah has given the Qur'an: "Then We have given the Book for inheritance to such of Our servants as We have chosen" (35:32). It is therefore wrong and indeed nonsensical to exclude people from the fold of Islam and the Ummah simply because they have wronged themselves. It is equally wrong to fail to recognize and admit such classification and to treat people as if they are all foremost in good deeds. Consequently, enthusiastic young Muslims should not hasten to accuse other Muslims of *fisq*, to show animosity and antipathy towards them simply because they have committed some minor sins, or some acts on which judgement is obscure and on which there is contradicting evidence.[46]

---

46 *IA*, p.132.

Moreover, Allah says in the Qur'an (4:31, 53:31-32) that He will forgive the small faults of those who avoid major sins, and may forgive even major sins of those who repent. It is therefore not fitting for human beings to pursue each others' weakness out of bigotry and zealotry. *Khalīfa*[47] 'Umar (RAA)[48] spoke firmly against a group of people who urged his Islamic Government to pursue people for minor sins—how much less are self-righteous individuals or cliques or committees empowered to do so!

In this context I wish to say something about *ḥijāb*. It is in my view quite wrong to use the first outward and visible sign of a Muslim woman, which is *ḥijāb*, as a clear indicator of whether she is a good or a bad Muslim. Some people seem to take the view that for women's dress, the blacker the better—if she is in black from head to toe she must be highly dedicated. If she wears socks too she must be even more dedicated. On the other hand if she wears European clothes she must be a very bad Muslim, if indeed she is a Muslim at all! This is a very simplistic analysis. It does not take into account the family background from which she has come. It may be that nobody in her household ever wore *hijāb*. It does not take into account the schools where she spent a minimum of thirteen years before going for higher education—in which schools European dress and physical education shorts and T-shirts were worn year after year in the presence of male teachers, male students and the general public. It does not take into account the strong influence of the media, the advertising business, the youth culture, which might have dominated her thinking throughout adolescence. It does not take into consideration that in some parts of the world—and not only non-Muslim parts—a woman in *ḥijāb* would find it difficult or impossible to get a job or even a place in a higher educational institution. All these factors and several others affect a Muslim girl's attitude to dress.

---

47 *khalīfa* (pl. *khulafā'*): Vicegerent of Allah in space-time. *Khilāfah*: The institution of man as vicegerent of Allah; the institution of government as continuation of the worldly government of the Prophet Muhammad.

48 RAA: *radiyah allahu 'anhu/'anha* May Allah be pleased with him/her. Said whenever a companion of the Prophet is mentioned by name.

Are we to look on all such women and girls as failures, who are not proper Muslims? From my own thirty years experience of knowing Muslim women from many parts of the world, I have been struck by the observation that some who dress decently but do not wear anything resembling *ḥijāb* could have a greater love of Allah, a greater devotion to prayers, a greater moral restraint and a greater degree of kindness to their fellow human beings than many who wear complete *ḥijāb* but have some other defects which, because they are not visible, may not be readily noticed.

Therefore we should not judge sternly by outer appearances but welcome all Muslim women to Islamic gatherings without conditions of dress, and without constantly nagging them about it. It is our duty to ensure that every Muslim woman is aware of the requirements of Islamic dress, the reasons for it and their importance. We should also encourage her to comply, using the Islamic principles of *ḥikmah,* i.e. wisdom and tact. It also helps if we can make available styles of dress that the ordinary woman finds acceptable which comply with Islamic principles. Ultimately she must make her own decision. We have to understand that every human being is on a journey and passes through different stages of spiritual and intellectual development. If we want such women to come close to keen Muslims and learn about Islam we have to understand them as they are now. If we reject them or show signs of looking down on them, they are likely to exercise their faculty of choice and avoid us in future. That would be a loss to themselves and a loss to the Ummah. We have to encourage those in full *ḥijāb* and those in semi-*ḥijāb* and those not in *ḥijāb*. Allah stated in the verse quoted earlier that the "servants He has chosen" include not just "the foremost in deeds" but also those who "follow a middle course" and "those who wrong their own souls". We are not set up as judges of other peoples' weaknesses.

I sometimes hear people say: "There are no half measures in Islam" which seems to mean: "You must be a perfect Muslim or you are nowhere". That is not possible, because even the best of Muslims only attained that status through a series of gradual stages of religious development.

Some people may ask: "Why should we not make a fuss about *ḥijāb*? Is it not compulsory in the Qur'an?"

Yes, it is, but so are a number of other things about which people are negligent. Even in the matter of dress, it is prescribed in the hadith for Muslim men to cover themselves in public from the navel to the knee. Yet, throughout the Muslim world, Muslim boys and young men come out for sports in brief shorts that do not reach even half way down the thigh. No one says they are going around naked. No one says such young men are disobeying Allah and His Messenger and should not attend Islamic activities.

In another example, the Qur'an has outlawed the giving and taking of *riba*[49] in the strongest terms. It warns that those who do not give it up should "take notice of war from Allah and his Prophet" (2:279). The hadith backs this up with a curse on those who take *riba*, those who give it and those who write and witness transactions involving it.

Yet countless Muslims the world over receive and pay interest on their bank accounts, and thousands work in banks. Our efforts to provide alternative ways of interest-free banking have been very feeble. Nobody suggests that those who give, take and witness interest on their bank accounts are not proper Muslims who are openly disobeying Allah. Nobody makes them feel unworthy to attend Islamic gatherings.

I am not saying that one wrongdoing justifies another wrongdoing. I am only pointing out that just as the young men are not conscious of offending against the Islamic code of dress by wearing brief shorts, and most bank-users are not conscious of offending against the Qur'anic prohibition of *riba*, so the Muslim girls unconsciously got used to inadequate dressing mainly during their time in school. There is no reason to be severe with them yet lenient with the others. The ultimate solution lies in insistence on proper dress for Muslim school girls and boys, and availability

---

49 *riba*: Interest on the value of money or commodity borrowed or used.

of interest-free banks. These are responsibilities that lie on all of us.

Allah's Sunan

Young people are generally in a hurry, and **haste** is a characteristic of mankind in general as mentioned in the Qur'an. Youth wants to sow today and harvest the next day—whereas it is a part of Allah's sunnah that all things take their time to mature, bear fruit and ripen.

Some young Muslims declare that they are ready to sacrifice their lives for the cause of Islam, and maybe they are. But in most cases it is not their lives that are required, but patient endeavour. Unfortunately very few are ready for the steady self-discipline of serious studies in order to attain excellence and uncover new truths in their fields of study. Many forget that "the pen is mightier than the sword" in its long-term effects. Mere sacrifice of lives cannot realize goals in the absence of well-planned, well thought-out strategies. Thus they seek an instant victory or martyrdom and refuse to undertake the pursuit of knowledge which requires unflinching perseverance over years, if not decades. They want 'an Islamic state' at once. But even if they had the means to impose it, where are the Muslims equipped with the knowledge and the intellectual and moral qualities to administer an Islamic State?

Rather, we have to truly cultivate ourselves as a broad Muslim community, to develop our natural potential and harness it so that our Ummah thinks and acts in an Islamic way. This requires a lot of patient work.

Some people object to this, thinking that patience would go on forever without achievement of the goal. Al Qaradawi responds:

> But, do you not in the meantime instruct an ignorant person, guide someone to the right path, or lead another to repent?...

This is a tremendous achievement which brings us closer to our goal.[50]

The Qur'an says:

And say: Work [righteousness]: Soon will Allah observe your work, and His Apostle, and the believers. Soon will you be brought back to the Knower of what is hidden and what is open. Then will He show you the truth of all that you did (9:105).

Honoring and Respecting True Scholarship

Muslim youth should respect expertise in the field of Islamic Studies as they respect it in other disciplines. A person does not become an expert in science by taking it for "A" level and reading a few books and magazines about it. It is not advisable to accept *fatāwā* from people who have inadequate qualifications to deliver them. In spite of the depth of knowledge of the Righteous *khulafā'*, they used to consult and be consulted by their learned companions when confronted with new and critical issues. 'Umar often used to reply, when asked for a fatwa, that he did not know.

Imam Malik used to say: "If a person is asked on a certain issue, he should think of *Jannah* [Heaven] and *Jahannam* [Hell] and of his own salvation in the hereafter before he replies." This reflects the hadith where the Prophet said that a person who guides other people to do right will share in the reward of their doing it, and a person who guides other people to wrong will share in their punishment if they do it.

We should give respect to those scholars who show humility, and recognize the need for proper training and study before anyone is qualified to exercise ijtihad[51]. Skill in rhetoric should

---

50 *IA*, p.145.

51 ijtihad: Considering that the accepted juridical sources of Islam are valid for all times and places, ijtihad may be described as a creative but disciplined intellectual effort to derive legal rulings from those sources while taking into

not be confused with knowledge of fiqh[52], and the person who excels in one may not excel in the other.

Shaikh al Qaradawi notes that a characteristic of a truly learned person is balance.

> Al Hasan al Basri warned us that "religion will be lost as a result of the practice of both the excessive and the negligent." The former tend to prohibit almost everything while the latter make everything lawful and permissable... We therefore need those balanced people who have the mind of a *faqīh*, and the heart of a pious man; those who can reconcile duties with reality, who distinguish clearly between what is to be expected from the less committed and what is to be expected of the committed.[53].

Da'wah: A Question of Tact and Wisdom

In their conduct of *da'wah* young Muslims should observe the ways of *da'wah* prescribed in the Qur'an (16:125;22:68-9 and 29:46) in a gracious manner, without wrangling, and with emphasis on points of common belief before discussion of areas of difference.

Likewise in conducting *da'wah* among Muslims the Prophet was told in the Qur'an:

> It is part of the mercy of Allah that you deal gently with them. If you were severe or hard-hearted, they would have broken away from you... (3:159).

There is a warning in this to those who like to go to extremes

---

consideration the variables imposed by the fluctuating circumstances of Muslim society.

52 fiqh: Knowledge of Islam through its laws; science of the law of Islam. *Faqīh* (pl. *fuqahā'*): A specialist in fiqh. Also can be a synonym for *'alim* (pl. ulama) meaning Islamic scholar. *Uṣūl al fiqh*: Science of Islamic jurisprudence, or the methodology of deriving laws from the sources of Islamic laws and of establishing their juristic or constitutional validity.

53 *IA*, p.154.

and try to enforce these extremes on others. Some of these fiery individuals are just fiery and quarrelsome by nature. If they had adopted Christianity they would have been fiery Christians; if they had adopted atheism they would have been fiery atheists. Every religion or ideology has its extremists. One should therefore not be browbeaten and bullied by such harsh preachers. They are already victims of their anger, their sternness and their wish to reprove others for their sins. And these characteristics often mar not only their preaching but also their manners in general as well as their relationship with other people, the politeness they should show to their elders and the respect they should give to people with greater knowledge, which may be concealed by natural humility.

They have forgotten the hadith that cheerfulness towards other people, even a smile, is a *ṣadaqah*[54] to be rewarded by Allah. They have forgotten the hadith from Aisha that "Allah is kind and loves kindness; and confers upon kindness what He does not confer upon severity and does not confer upon anything else beside it"[55]. Aisha did not forget such *aḥādīth*, and several times she mentioned occasions when the Prophet corrected her for an excess of youthful severity or impatience.

Idealism, Daydreams and the Immediate Task

Shaikh al Qaradawi urges that rather than indulging in idealistic daydreams of a perfect world, it would be better for us to be more realistic and grapple with the problems of people here and now, to act with a view to solving the daily suffering and needs of impoverished, dispossessed and alienated masses in our countryside and urban centers who lack a decent education and even the basics of life and health.

> They must come down to earth and identify with the masses, those who live from hand to mouth in the downtrodden parts

---

54 *ṣadaqah* (pl. *ṣadaqāt*): Voluntary almsgiving.
55 Reported by Muslim.

> of the big cities and in the impoverished and totally forgotten villages. In such places one can find the uncorrupted sources of virtue, simplicity and purity in spite of "necessity's sharp pinch." There one can find the potential for social change, the opportunities for effort, struggle, movement, help, and reconstruction; there one can mix with the masses and show kindness and compassion towards the needy, the orphaned, the brokenhearted, the weary, and the oppressed. The realization of such objectives, which is in itself a form of *'ibādah*, requires collective effort, the formation of committees dedicated to eradicating illiteracy, diseases, unemployment, lack of initiative, and harmful habits.[56]

These are individual and collective duties which are a suitable form of *'ibādah* for those who wish to see the Muslim Ummah drag itself out of the mud of its decline.

In Shaikh al Qaradawi's view, it is the experience of serving one's own community that will

> mould, prepare and test the abilities of future generations for the leadership of the Ummah. It is unacceptable for a Muslim who could, if he so wished, provide a cure for a patient at a public clinic or charitable hospital to refuse to do because he is waiting for an Islamic state to be established and provide such services.[57]

Thus there must be long-term preparation leading to ultimate objectives, but also a lot of hard work to meet immediate needs and alleviate immediate ills.

Belief in Human Goodness

Shaikh al Qaradawi ends his book with advice to young Muslims to

> liberate themselves from pessimism, and assume innocence

---

56 *IA*, p.161.
57 *IA*, p.163.

> and goodness in fellow-Muslims. We need a sympathetic understanding of people's weaknesses and faults, because they are a part of human nature.[58]

This requires a high degree of awareness together with the acknowledgement that no one but Allah knows a person's innermost thoughts and motives, and that we must judge people by what they profess, not by what we suspect. The Qur'an, as mentioned earlier, tells us that "some suspicion is a sin".

We must also recognize that every believer in Allah and His messenger cannot be devoid of some inborn good, however evil his practice may be. The Prophet used to treat wrong-doers as a physician would treat a patient, not as a policeman would treat a criminal.

In these ways the bond of Muslim brotherhood and sisterhood is not severed but strengthened. We need as ever to study and follow the exemplary pattern that the Prophet set up for us.

Those extremists who indiscriminately accuse whoever makes a mistake of *kufr* or *shirk* must understand that they have to change their outlook and strategy and learn that a great deal of the corruption and perversion that they abhor results mainly from ignorance or bad company. A wise man once said: 'Rather than cursing darkness, try to light a candle for the road'.

Before reaching my own conclusions on this issue there are some related points which I wish to cover with my Nigerian experience in mind.

Extremism: An Impediment to *Da'wah*

Two points are worth dealing with at this level:

The **first** point is the broad question of *da'wah* and the effects

---

58 *IA*, p.164.

of extremism on it. Does extremism benefit the cause of *da'wah* or harm it? I think there is no doubt that it harms it for a number of reasons.

Firstly, extremism is by its definition a position taken by a minority—those that are far from the center or middle of the road. Therefore an extremist attitude will not attract the majority of non-Muslims, who would simply find it too difficult to follow. Nor is it likely to appeal to the majority of Muslims, for the same reason.

Secondly, extremism hinders *da'wah* by causing unnecessary conflicts which in turn cause concern to people in authority or give them reason to intervene. People in power are naturally sensitive to instability, and will readily impose restrictions to prevent any recurrence of it. These restrictions limit the freedom of serious *da'wah* organizations to carry out their programs. To give a simple example, a few years ago in Nigeria a group of extremists began visiting a girls' boarding school taking advantage of the freedom of the Muslim Students Society and other organizations to conduct religious lectures at weekends. After a while it was learned that there was trouble. These enthusiasts had convinced some of the Muslim girls that they should refuse to attend classes in *kufr* knowledge and should abandon their education so as to go and get married. The school authorities, the parents, the Ministry of Education, religious leaders and even the former State Governor became involved in sorting the matter out. The outcome was that the Ministry of Education directed that no outside preachers or religious lecturers should be allowed into any of the schools in the whole State. Therefore not only the Muslim Students Society but other reputable Islamic organizations were obliged to suspend all their programs designed to enlighten the secondary school students about Islam. This is one example among many of how extremists could abuse the freedom that exists in a country, as a result of which that freedom could be denied to all.

It is a truism that for the past five decades or so many regimes in the Muslim world have been bent on de-Islamizing Muslim society in the name of concepts inimical to it. As a result, they have put severe restrictions on religious education and *da'wah* activities. One of these restrictions is the introduction of the preaching permit. This official violence has been a major cause of extremism. Yet, in such countries as Nigeria, anyone used to be free to preach anywhere in the country; but when **some** Muslims abused that freedom through sheer excess of zeal and bigotry, *da'wah* work suffered a great deal because nobody was then allowed to preach without having to go through an elaborate process of screening to get a permit. Therefore extremism often constitutes a great obstacle to serious *da'wah.*

Islam in itself is quite clearly the front runner as a religion acceptable to the majority of mankind.

Its teachings about the unity of God, the brotherhood of mankind and the accountability of human beings for their actions are clear, reasonable, good and true. Its scripture, the Qur'an, is well-authenticated and not subject to doubt. Its acts of worship—*ṣalāh*, *ṣiyām*, *zakāh* and the ḥajj help to purify and discipline a person, and its moral teachings foster love, sharing and cooperation between people of all races. This is the religion that many ordinary people all over the world are quietly searching for, the one that strikes the perfect balance between this life and the hereafter.

But if some Muslims through their own excesses and public statements fail to demonstrate the beauty of Islam, and portray it as a religion of difficulty, internal strife, harshness or aggression, then non-Muslims will either run away or oppose us, because they find us oppressive, unreasonable and frightening.

The **second** point I wish to touch on is the use of the word *kāfirūn* (unbelievers) to describe Christians and Jews. We should remind ourselves that the Qur'an consistently addresses them as *ahl al kitāb* (People of the Book)—people to whom revelation has come and who know something about Allah and His unity, even if they have some other doctrines that have distorted or clouded the straight path. *Kāfirūn* in the Qur'an refers to idol-worshippers and those who refused to believe in God or the Day of Judgement. *Ahl al kitāb* were always distinct and enjoyed a protected status within the Islamic State. The continued survival of Jewish and Christian communities in Arab and Muslim lands until the present time is a witness to the tolerance extended to them by Muslims.

Therefore it is not justified to label all non-Muslims as *kāfirūn*. Nor is it correct to say that the Christians at the time the Qur'an was revealed were not compromising the Unity of God. The Qur'an mentions the erroneous beliefs of some Christians about the Trinity, and about the Prophet 'Isa as God, or as Son of God, and describes these beliefs as "a denial of the truth" (5:73). Yet it still refers to them as *ahl al kitāb*, and still mentions that among them are some who are closest in affection to the Muslims (5:82). Asad comments on this verse:

> Although, by their deification of Jesus, they are guilty of *shirk* ("the ascribing of divinity to anyone or anything beside God"), the Christians do not *consciously* worship a plurality of deities in-as-much as, theoretically, their theology postulates belief in the One God, who is conceived as manifesting himself in a trinity of aspects, "persons", of whom Jesus is supposed to be one. However repugnant this doctrine may be to the teachings of the Qur'an, their *shirk* is not based on conscious intent, but rather flows from their "overstepping the bounds of truth" in their veneration of Jesus (see Qur'an 4:171 and 5:77).[59]

Muslims must of course protect themselves and their faith against aggression and subversion from any quarter, but they should not go beyond what the Qur'an permits in labelling all non-Muslims as *kāfirūn*. Why give offence and achieve nothing? It is in conditions of peace that Islam spreads most rapidly, as could be seen after the Treaty of Hudaybiya. The Peace allowed the Muslims to move freely among the non-Muslims and to carry the message of Islam to them. As a result, within a few years time there was no need to fight for Makkah because the Muslims

---

59 Note 97, p.160, *The Message of the Qur'an*, Translated and Explained by Muhammad Asad, Dar Al-Andalus, Gibraltar, 1980.

had already become more numerous than the pagans.

From what is recorded of the deeds of the Prophet it is clear that he regarded all non-Muslims as potential Muslims, and exercised a lot of patience in calling them to Islam, whether they were Jews, Christians or pagans. Today many non-Muslims are ready to embrace Islam if we are ready to call them and teach them in the manner we are told to do it in the Qur'an—with *ḥikmah* and gracious preaching, and by cogent reasoning.

If we do this, sincerely and patiently, and avoid regarding ourselves as two rival football teams, Muslims versus Christians, there is every prospect of success; because if we do things that Allah commands us in the way He has commanded us, He has promised ultimate success, whatever the setbacks on the way.

I am convinced that the truth cannot be suppressed for long. Some Christian leaders, for example, may try to cause their followers to hate Muslims and Islam. There are recent examples of their deliberately spreading misinformation about Islam in booklets and by word of mouth so that their followers would close their minds to it and refuse to listen when Muslims try to inform them. There are cases I have witnessed of educated Christians refusing to touch a piece of paper containing some facts about Islam, or literally putting their fingers in their ears rather than hear anything about it.

However, not all the followers are like sheep, and many are ready to use their independent judgment if they can see for themselves that the truth is other than what they were told. I have met many converts to Islam who said that the main reason for their conversion was that they liked the way Muslims behaved, or that they experienced some acts of kindness and sincerity from a Muslim or that a Muslim got into conversation with them and explained Islam in a way they could understand.

So our manner of approach to all non-Muslims (as well as to Muslims) is very important. Each person is different. Until you have engaged an individual in conversation you do not know what he believes and why he believes it, and whether he is satisfied with his present beliefs. And if you start with a hostile or scornful attitude you will get nowhere. You will only succeed in confirming what he might have been told about Muslims being aggressive. Our task is to remove the prejudices, not to confirm them. Whoever confirms those prejudices and drives non-Muslims away is doing a disservice to Islam, to the Muslim Ummah and to mankind who are waiting for true guidance while some of those who have this guidance are preoccupied with quarrelling among themselves and failing to convey the message to those who have not heard it.

Status of Western Languages

The younger generation of Muslims seem to be more noisily anti-colonialist than their parents who actually experienced colonial rule. In spite of around thirty years of political independence, some youth tend to blame all our misfortunes on the "former colonial masters". Of course it must be stated that colonialism was inherently wrong, and Europeans had no right to seize and exploit other countries' peoples and wealth. But to blame all current ills on colonialism is going too far, and is often a convenient way of avoiding honest discussion of some home-grown bad habits.[60]

This colonial association is probably the basis for some of our students reacting against the English and French languages as means of communication. Some say to use them is a mark of slavery. It is understandable for people to prefer to use, among themselves, their native language, in which they feel as natural as a fish in water. It is natural for some to feel embarrassed about

60 This is one of the basic arguments in Malek Bennabi's thinking. The late Algerian Muslim thinker consistently argued that while colonialism was responsible for the Ummah's problems until independence was achieved, the absence of a "super-effort" to get over those problems reflects "colonisability", that is a mental attitude that favors continued colonialism in various aspects. (Eds.)

their inadequate command of a foreign language. It is natural to feel there is something wrong with an African speaking to another African in a European tongue. However, such feelings should be governed by reason. Some Nigerian Muslim students in Northern universities have recently been insisting on conducting their activities in the mosque in Hausa. The outcome is the departure of the Muslims who do not speak Hausa to other mosques. What of Islamic unity and brotherhood? Which is more important: the Hausa language or the unity of Muslims?

Secondly, the colonial legacy of the English and French languages as media of international communication has brought some advantages to Muslims in the modern world. It has offered tremendous opportunities for the exchange of ideas and co-operation between Muslims all over the world. We might have preferred Arabic to play that role, but historical development dictated otherwise.

Meanwhile at international Islamic conferences it is common to find a majority of papers in English or French. There is now a vast and ever-increasing literature on Islam in these languages written by Muslims. Muslims in countries like Nigeria where tribes speak different languages (Hausa, Yoruba, Ibo and so on) can understand one another and come closer through the common English language. The common use of English and French as linguistic tools or as means of communication and of *da'wah* by various parts of the Ummah is a necessity of modern life. Muslims from many parts of the world can exchange visits, research and information because of having English or French as a common linguistic medium.

English in particular has become an international language of Islam. Yusuf Ali's translation of the Qur'an has encircled the globe. And there are vast opportunities for *da'wah* in the English and French-speaking countries where Muslims have settled as minorities.

It may also be remembered that other languages have been "Islamized" in the past. Persian was once the language of the

Zoroastrians, but it became the medium for a highly-developed Islamic literature, including the religious poetry of such masters as Jalaluddin Rumi. Hausa in Nigeria was in the past a language of pagans, but over the centuries of the spread of Islam it took in many Arabic expressions and loan words.

If Muslims living in the West begin to express themselves in English and develop their own prose and poetry in English expressing Islamic thought, the English language itself can change as it has changed continuously for hundreds of years to reflect new influences. Language is never static. Allah moreover refers to differences of language, color and tribe as among His signs and blessings (Qur'an 3:22; 40:13).

Therefore rather than adopting a parochial and negative attitude, using English and French reluctantly, calling them languages of the *kuffār* and refusing to learn them well, we would surely do better to adopt a realistic approach and take every opportunity to master them for the benefit of Islam and the Muslims. This does not mean dropping one's own language, but being fluently bi-lingual or tri-lingual.

Correcting Evil-Doing

Consider the following hadith:

> If you see evil-doing you should change it with your hand; and if that is not possible, change it with your tongue, and if that is not possible, reject it in your heart: and that is the weakest of faith.[61]

Some people have misunderstood this hadith as a challenge to their manly courage. They understand it to mean that those of strong faith and courage should boldly use force to correct evil-doing, those who have less faith and courage should at least speak against evil while those of the least faith and courage should at

---

61 Reported by al Nawawi.

least inwardly reject and abjure the evil. Therefore they conclude that the use of force is superior to speaking against evil-doing, and is ideally the first course of action.

This cannot however be what the hadith means. We are aware that the Prophet preached among evil-doers in Makkah for thirteen years and to the best of our knowledge never once attempted to use force to correct them. Some of his followers were tortured and killed; his response was to send others to a place of safety in Abyssinia. But we could never say that these responses indicated lack of faith or courage. These were signs of his realistic understanding that to fight back at that time would be suicidal to his cause. He was not in a position to stop oppression with his hand. To have done so would have only brought disaster on himself and the defenceless Muslims. Therefore he continued preaching and speaking courageously against the evil-doing of the idol-worshippers and had faith that the situation would change in God's good time. Events proved him right.

Muslims are not to act without common sense and prudence. This advice is contained in the hadith: "Trust in God but tie your camel."[62]

A good general knows that he may have to concede some territory or even lose a battle in order to win a war. We should not allow local and transient events to divert us from long-term objectives.

Even in Madinah, where the Prophet possessed political leadership, he always preferred persuasion to force. There are a number of *aḥādīth* dealing with wrong-doers brought to the Prophet. 'Umar or some other Companions would request the Prophet to authorize putting them to death or inflicting upon them some major punishment. He would refuse, and instead draw the person close and speak to him quietly of the moral and spiritual issues involved in his conduct, in such a way that he would

---

62 *Al-Muwaṭṭa.*

understand and reform himself.

If we look at the hadith with these examples of the Prophet in mind, it can be seen to offer another meaning:

> If you see evil-doing and are in a position to correct it (that is, you have the authority or ability to stop it) then you should exercise that authority, even to the extent of using a measure of force if necessary.
>
> If you do not possess the authority to stop the evil-doing, but are in a position to warn against it, or call on the authorities concerned to stop it, or mobilize public opinion against it, you have a moral duty to do so.
>
> If you are in a position where you cannot even report to the authorities or even raise your voice without being crushed, and have no means of migrating from the evil situation, you still have the obligation to continue to reject and denounce the evil-doing in your heart.

In other words whatever your level of authority or ability to correct evil-doing, you have a moral duty to exercise it as far as you are capable, and should not neglect it, because it is part of commanding what is good and forbidding what is wrong, which is the characteristic of a Muslim community.

To put the situation in a familiar context, it may be that a college Students Union is planning a contest to choose a beauty queen. Committed Muslim students are naturally strongly opposed to it, but are outvoted. The contest is to go ahead. What should they do?

Perhaps they appeal to the college authorities to step in and forbid it (using their tongues to correct evil-doing). The authorities reply that it is a students' affair and they cannot interfere, or that it is a multi-religious institution, and so on.

So what next? Are they to use their hands to destroy the musical instruments and short-circuit all the lights on the night of the contest? It could be done, and has been done. But what is the likely outcome? For unlawful destruction of university property the students could be dismissed or even imprisoned. Then they have become the enemies of those who wanted to enjoy the beauty contest. Next time there is a Muslim Students Society function some of the other students may come and short-circuit the lights or destroy the loud speaker in revenge. Meanwhile the beauty contest is re-scheduled and takes place the following week with stricter security precautions against sabotage. Did those who tried to change things with their hands without authority gain or lose, on balance?

What else could they have done? Firstly, have they been carrying on effective *da'wah* among the Muslim students all along, so that if they happen to be a majority they could outvote others in the Students Union? Secondly, if they could not raise a majority against it, has their *daw'ah* among the Muslim sisters been widespread and effective enough to ensure that no Muslim girl takes part in the competition? Thirdly, what of using prayer time at the college mosques to counsel Muslim students against attendance? Fourthly, what of using the campus newspaper to explain why they think beauty contests are degrading? Fifthly, what of organizing an alternative interesting activity at another venue to coincide with the beauty contest? Sixthly, there is the option of paying attention to their studies so that in 10-20 years' time they could become the lecturers, professors and ultimately the university authorities themselves, in which event they would wield a great deal of legitimate influence not only over students' entertainments but also the whole running of the institution with all the scope for healthy change?

I suggest we reflect for a moment on the career of Mikhail Gorbachev of the Soviet Union. He rose steadily through the Communist ranks under a succession of diehard Communist presidents. He became the head of the KGB—the Soviet Security apparatus. Yet when it was his turn to occupy the top post, he astonished people by dismantling the Soviet empire in Eastern Europe and introducing reforms that started off the end of communism. If he had dared to express his views 10 or 20 years ago he would have been finished before coming anywhere near to power.

I am not suggesting that Muslims should conceal their Islamic identity, but that they should not try to exert authority over others, an authority which they do not rightly possess, nor should they take illegal action which could result in frustration of their long-term aims of reform.

Those who are serious about Islamization and *da'wah* must be clear about their methods, which must accord with Islamic teachings. There are all sorts of ways of bringing about change that are far more successful than force or threat of force. But they need clear thinking, balanced judgment, love of truth, hard work, initiative, patience and confidence in Allah's support.

By studying the Islamic sources we can see that moderation and balance are at the heart of the religion. They are not to be equated with half-hearted commitment to Islam, but are the true and authentic expression of the faith in accordance with the Qur'an and the life-example of the Prophet. These are manifested in kindness and good manners, and a reasoned approach to *da'wah*.

I hope that what I have said, or quoted from the Qur'an and the hadith or from the comments of Shaikh al Qaradawi, will be of use to committed Muslims and a source of guidance in their approach to life now and in the future. If I have made any mistakes I pray Allah to forgive me and hope for correction from those with more knowledge.

Publications of the IIIT

A. Accessing the Islamic Intellectual Heritage

ARABIC
Kitāb al Ilm li Ahmad ibn Shu'ayb al Nasa'i [Al Nasa'i's Book of Knowledge] (1413/1993) a study and enquiry by Faruq Hamadah.

B. Dissertations Series

ARABIC
Al Khiṭāb al 'Arabi al Mu'āsir: Qira'ah Naqdiyah fi Mafāhīm al Nahḍah wa al Taqaddum wa al Ḥadāthah [The Contemporary Arab Discourse: A Critical Study of the Concepts of Renaissance, Progress and Modernisation 1978-1987] (1411/1991) by Fadi Ismail.

Al Maqāsid al 'Āmmah li al Sharī'ah al Islāmiyah [General Objectives of the Shari'ah] by Yusuf Hamid Alim.

Manhaj al Baḥth al Ijtimā'i Bayna al Waḍ'iyah wa al Mi'yāriyah [Social Research Methodology] (1411/1991) by Muhammad Muhammad Imiziyan.

Naẓariyat al Maqāṣid 'Inda al Imām al Shatībī [The Theory of Objectives According to Imām al Shaṭībī] (1411/1991) by Ahmad al Raysūni.

Nazariyāt al Tanmiyah al Siyāsiyah al Mu'āṣirah: Dirāsah Naqdiyah Muqāranah fi Daw' al Manẓūr al Haḍarī al Islāmi [Contemporary Political Development Theories: A Comparative Critical Analysis from an Islamic Civilizational Perspective] by Nasr Muhammad 'Arif.

Al Qur'an wa al Naẓar al 'Aqlī [The Qur'an and Reasoning] by Fatimah I.M. Isma'il.

C. Human Development Series

ENGLISH
Training Guide for Islamic Workers (1411/1991) by Dr Hisham Altalib. Editions in Arabic, French, Turkish and Malaysian forthcoming.

D. Indices Series

ARABIC
Al Kashshāf al Iqtiṣādi li Āyāt al Qur'an al Karīm [Economic Index of the Qur'an] (1411/1991) by Muhyi al Din 'Atiyah.

Al Fikr al Tarbawi al Islāmi: Qā'imah Bibliyughrāfiyah [Islamic Educational Thought: A Bibliography] (1412/1992) by Muhyi al Din 'Atiyah.

Al Kashshāf al Maḍū'i li Ṣaḥīḥ al Bukhāri [Index to *Ṣaḥiḥ al Bukhāri*] by Muhyi al Din 'Atiyah.

Qā'imah Mukhtārah Ḥawla al Ma'rifah wa al Fikr wa al Manhaj wa al Thaqāfah, wa al Haḍārah [Selected list of articles in the Social Sciences] (1413/1992) by Muhyi al Din 'Atiyah.

E. Islamic Methodology Series

ARABIC
Azmat al 'Aql al Muslim [The Crisis of Muslim Thought] (1411/1991) by AbdulHamīd AbūSulaymān.

Al Manhajiyah al Islāmiyah wa al 'Ulūm al Sulūkiyah wa al Tarbawiyah: Buhūth wa Munāqashat al Mu'tamar al 'Ālami al Rābi' li al Fikr al Islāmi [Islamic Methodology and the Behavioral and Educational Sciences], Vol. 1 (1411 /1990) edited by al Taib Zayn al 'Abidin.

Al Manhajiyah al Islāmiyah wa al 'Ulūm al Sulūkiyah [Islamic Methodology and the Behavioral and Educational Sciences], Vol. 2 edited by al Taib Zayn al 'Abidin.

Al Manhajiyah al Islāmiyah wa al 'Ulūm al Sulūkiyah [Islamic Methodology and the Behavioral and Educational Sciences], Vol. 3 edited by al Taib Zayn al 'Abidin.

Ma'ālim al Manhaj al Islāmi [Outlines of Islamic Methodology] (1411/1990) by Muhammad 'Imarah.

Khilafat al Insān Bayna al Wahī wa al 'Aql: Bahth fi Jadaliyat al Nass wa al 'Aql wa al Waqi' [The Vicegerency of Man] (1413/1993) by 'Abd al Majid al Najjar.

F. Islamization of Culture Series

ARABIC
Dalīl Maktabat al Usrah al Muslimah [Guide to Literature for the Muslim Family] (1405/1985). Planned and supervised by Dr AbdulHamīd AbūSulaymān.

G. Islamization of Knowledge Series

ARABIC
Islāmiyyat al Ma'rifah [Islamization of Knowledge], (1406/1986).

Naḥwa Niẓām Naqdi 'Ādil [Toward A Just Monetary System], 2nd edition, (1409/1989) by Dr Muhammad 'Umar Chapra.

Al Wajīz fī Islāmiyat al Ma'rifah [Synopsis of Islamization of Knowledge] (1408/1987).

Naḥwa 'Ilm al Insān al Islāmi: Ta'rif wa Naẓariyāt wa Ittijahāt. A translation of *Toward Islamic Anthropology* (1409/1989) by Dr Akbar S. Ahmed.

Turāthunā al Fikrī fī Mizān al Shar' wa al 'Aql [Our Intellectual Legacy Under the Scrutiny of Law and Reason] (1411/1991) by Muhammad Ghazali.

Madkhal ila Islāmiyat al Mar'ifah Ma'a Mukhattat Muqtaraḥ li Islāmiyat 'Ilm al Tārīkh [Introduction to Islamization of Knowledge and Proposals for the Islamization of History] (1411/1991) by 'Imad al Din Khalil.

Iṣlāh al Fikr al Islāmi Bayna al Qudurāt wa al 'Aqabāt—Waraqat 'Amal [Reforming Islamic Thought: Capabilities and Obstacles—A Working Paper] (1411/1991) by Dr. Ṭāhā J. al 'Alwānī.

Al Qur'an wa al Nazar al 'Aqlī [The Qur'an and Reasoning] by Fatimah I.M. Isma'il.

ENGLISH
The Islamic Theory of International Relations: New Directions for Islamic Methodology and Thought (1411/1987) by Dr AbdulHamīd AbūSulaymān.

Islamization of Knowledge: General Principles and Work Plan, 3rd edition (1409 /1989).

Toward Islamic Anthropology: Definitions, Dogma, and Directions (1406/1986) by Dr Akbar S. Ahmad.

Toward Islamic English (1406/1986) by Dr Ismā'īl R. al Fārūqī. Jointly produced by the Institute and the Muslim Students Association.

Modelling-Interest Free Economy: A Study in Microeconomics and Development (1407/1987) by Dr Muhammad Anwar.

Islam: Source and Purpose of Knowledge. Papers presented at the Second International Conference on Islamic Thought and the Islamization of Knowledge (1409/1988).

Toward the Islamization of Disciplines. Papers presented at the Third International Conference on Islamic Thought and the Islamization of Knowledge (1409/1989).

The Organisation of the Islamic Conference: An Introduction to an Islamic Political Institution (1408/1988) by Dr 'Abdullah al Ahsan.

Islamization of Attitudes and Practices in Science and Technology. Proceedings of the Workshop on the Islamization of Attitudes and Practices in Science and Technology. Edited by M.A.K. Lodhi (1407/1987).

Where East Meets West: The West on the Agenda of the Islamic Revival (1412/1992) by Dr Mona Abul-Fadl.

Qur'anic Concepts of Human Psyche. Edited by Zafar Afaq Ansari (1412/1992).

GERMAN

Das Einbringen des Islam in das Wissen: Allgemeine Grundsatze und Arbeitsplan. A translation of *Islamization of Knowledge: General Principles and Work Plan.* Jointly Produced by the Institute and Muslim Studenten Vereinigung e.V (1408/1988).

Fur Ein Islamisches Deutsch adapted from Dr Ismā'īl R. al Fārūqī's *Towards Islamic English* (1408/1988).

H. Issues in Islamic Thought Series

ARABIC

Hujjiyat al Sunnah [Legal Authoritativeness of the Sunnah], 1st edition, (1407 /1986) by Dr 'Abd al Ghani 'Abd al Khaliq.

Adab al Ikhtilāf fi al Islām [Ethics of Disagreement in Islam], 3rd edition (1407/1987) by Dr Ṭāhā J. al 'Alwānī. Published by permission of the Shari'ah Courts and Religious Affairs Administration of the State of Qatar. Also translated into Urdu, Bengali, and Malay; English and French translations forthcoming.

Al Ṣaḥwah al Islāmiyyah Bayna al Juhūd wa al Taṭarruf [Islamic Awakening Between Rejection and Extremism] (1403/1984) by Dr Yusuf al Qaradawi. Published by permission of the Shari'ah Courts and Religious Affairs Administration of the State of Qatar.

Al Islām wa al Tanmiyah al Ijtimā'iyah [Islam and Social Development], (1406 /1989) by Dr Muhsin Abd al Hamid.

Kayfah Nata'āmal Ma'a al Sunnah al Nabawiyyah [Methods of Understanding the Sunnah] 2nd Edition, (1411/1990), by Dr Yusuf al Qaradawi.

Kayfa Nata'āmal Ma'a al Qur'an [Methods of Understanding the Qur'an], (1411 /1991), a Dialogue Between Shaikh Muhammad al Ghazali and 'Umar 'Ubayd Hasanah.

Murāja'āt fi al Fikr wa al Da'wah wa al Ḥarakah [Re-examination in Islamic Thought, Daw'ah and Movement], (1412/1991), by 'Umar 'Ubayd Hasanah.

Hawla Tashkīl al 'Aql al Muslim [About the Formation of the Muslim Mind], (1412/1991), by 'Imad al Din Khalil.

Al Muslimūn wa al Badīl al Hadāri [The Muslims and the Civilizational Alternative], (1412/1992), by Haydar Abd al Karim Al Ghadir.

Mushkilatān Waqiraatān Fīhima [An Anatomy of Two Issues] (1412/1991), by A. Tariq al Bashiri.

Huqūq al Muwatanah: Huqūq Ghayr al Muslim fi al Mujtama' al Islāmi [The Rights of Citizenry: Minorities in Muslim Society] (1413/1993) by Rashid al Ghannoushi.

ENGLISH

Tawhīd: Its Implications for Thought and Life, Second Edition (1412/1992) by Dr. Ismā'īl R. al Fārūqī.

Islamic Thought and Culture, papers presented to the Islamic Studies Group of the American Academy of Religion (1402/1982). Edited by Dr. Ismā'īl R. al Fārūqī.

Essays in Islamic and Comparative Studies, papers presented to the Islamic Studies Group of the American Academy of Religion (1402/1982). Edited by Dr. Ismā'īl R. al Fārūqī.

Trialogue of the Abrahamic Faiths, 2nd edition (1406/1986). Papers presented to the Islamic Studies Group of the American Academy of Religion. Edited by Dr. Ismā'īl R. al Fārūqī.

Islamic Awakening: Between Rejection and Extremism, 2nd edition (1412/1991) by Dr Yusuf al Qaradawi. New edition revised and edited by Anas S. al Shaikh-Ali and Mohammed B. E. Wasfy. First edition 1407/1987. Published jointly with the American Trust Publications.

Madīnan Society at the Time of the Prophet: Its Characteristics and Organization, Vol.1, (1411/1991) by Dr Akram Diya' al 'Umari.

Madīnan Society at the Time of the Prophet: The Jihad against the Mushrikun, Vol.2, (1411/1991) by Dr Akram Diya' al 'Umari.

Ethics of Disagreement in Islam (1412/1992) by Dr. Ṭāhā J. al 'Alwānī.

I. Lectures Series

ARABIC

Al Azmah al Fikriyah al Mu'āsirah: [The Contemporary Intellectual Crisis], (1409/1989) by Dr Ṭāhā J. al 'Alwānī.

J. Occasional Papers Series

LONDON OFFICE

ENGLISH
Outlines of a Cultural Strategy (1410/1989) by Dr Ṭāhā J. al 'Alwānī.

Islamization of Knowledge: A Methodology (1412/1991) by Professor 'Imad al Din Khalil.

The Qur'an and the Sunnah: the Time-Space Factor (1412/1991) by Professor 'Imad al Din Khalil.

Ijtihad (1412/1992) by Dr Ṭāhā J. al 'Alwānī.

FRENCH
Pour Une Stratégie Culturelle Islamique (1411/1990) by Dr Ṭāhā J. al 'Alwānī.

Methodologie Pour L'Islamisation Du Savoir (1412/1991) by Professor 'Imad al Din Khalil.

Le Coran et la Sounna: le Facteur Temps-Espace (1412/1991) by Dr Ṭāhā J. al 'Alwānī and Professor 'Imad al Din Khalil.

L'Ijtihad (1412/1993) by Dr Ṭāhā J. al 'Alwānī.

GERMAN
Entwurf Eines Alternativen Kulturplanes [Outlines of a Cultural Strategy] (1412/1992) by Dr Ṭāhā J. al 'Alwānī.

PAKISTAN OFFICE

Knowledge: An Islamic Perspective (1412/1991) by Bakhtiar Husain Siddiqui.

Islamization of Knowledge - A Critical Overview (1412/1992) by Seyyed Vali Reza Nasr.

K. Perspectives on Islamic Thought Series

ENGLISH

National Security and Development Strategy: Towards an Integrated Strategy for the Defence and Development of Pakistan (1411/1990) by Arshad Zaman.

Nationalism and Internationalism in Liberalism, Marxism and Islam (1412/1991) by Tahir Amin.

L. Research Monographs Series

ARABIC

Usūl al Fiqh al Islāmi : Manhaj Bahth wa Ma'rifah [Sources of Islamic Jurisprudence: Methodology for Research and Knowledge] (1408/1988) by Dr Ṭāhā J. al 'Alwānī.

Al Tafakkur Min al Mushāhadah ilā al Shuhūd: Dirāsah Nafsiyah Islāmiyah [Contemplation: Observation and its Object] (1411/1991) by Dr Malik Badri.

Ruh al Hadārah al Islāmiyah [The Essence of the Muslim Civilization] (1411/1991) by Muhammad al Fadil ibn Ashur.

Falsafat al Tanmiyah: Ru'yah Islāmiyah [The Concept of Change in Islam] (1413/1992) by Ibrahim Ahmad 'Umar.

Al 'Ilm wa al Imān: Madkhal ila Nazariyat al Ma'rifah fi al Islam [Knowledge and Faith: an Introduction to Epistemology] (1412/1992) by Ibrahim Ahmad 'Umar.

Dawr Hurrīyat al Ra'y fi al Wahdah al Fikrīyah Bayna al Muslimīn [Role of Freedom of Thought among the Muslims] (1413/1992) by 'Abd al Majīd al Najjār.

ENGLISH

Usūl al Fiqh al Islami: Source Methodology in Islamic Jurisprudence (1411 /1991) by Dr Ṭaha Jabir al 'Alwani, edited by Y.T. DeLorenzo and Dr Anas S. al Shaikh-Ali.

Islam and the Middle East: The Aesthetics of a Political Inquiry (1411/1991) by Dr Mona AbulFadl.

The Geological Concept of Mountains in the Qur'an (1411/1990) by Z.R. El-Naggar.

M. Studies in the Islamization of Knowledge Series *[Rasa'il fi Islamiyat al Ma'rifah]*- Published by the Cairo Office.

ARABIC
Khawātir fi al Azmah al Fikriyah wa al Ma'zaq al Hadāri li al Ummah al Islāmiyyah [Thoughts on the Intellectual Crisis and the Civilizational Dilemma Facing the Muslim Ummah], No. 1 (1409/1989) by Dr Ṭāhā J. al 'Alwānī.

Nizām al Islam al 'Aqā'idi fi al 'Asr al Ḥadīth [Islam's System of Beliefs and the Modern Age], No. 2 (1409/1989) by Professor Muhammad al Mubarak.

Al Usus al Islamiyah li al 'Ilm [The Islamic Foundations of Science], No. 3 (1409/1989) by Dr Muhammad Mu'in Siddiqi.

Qadiyat al Manhajiyah fi al Fikr al Islāmi [The Issue of Methodology in Islamic Thought], No. 4 (1409/1989) by Dr AbdulHamīd AbūSulaymān.

Siyāghat al 'Ulūm al Ijtimā'iyah Siyāghah Islāmiyyah [On Islamizing the Social Sciences], No. 5 (1409/1989) by Dr Ismā'īl R. al Fārūqī.

Azmat al Ta'līm al Mu'āsir wa Hulūlūha al Islāmiyah [The Crisis in Contemporary Education: The Islamic Solution], No. 6 (1409/1989) by Dr Zaghlul Raghib al Najjar.

Madkhal ilā Islāmiyat al Ma'rifah [Introduction to the Islamization of Knowledge], No. 7 (1411/1990) by Dr 'Imad al Din Khalil.

N. Other Works

ARABIC
Kitāb al Mu'tamar al Tarbawi [The Education Conference Book] Edited by Dr. Fathi H. Malkawi. (1411/1990).

Bihūth al Mu'tamar al Tarbawi [The Education Conference Papers] Volume 1. Edited by Dr. Fathi H. Malkawi. (1411/1990).

Bihūth al Mu'tamar al Tarbawi [The Education Conference Papers] Volume 2. Edited by Dr. Fathi H. Malkawi. (1411/1991).

Al Ḥarakah al Islāmiyah fī Dilli al Tahawulāt al Dawliyah wa Azmat al Khalīj [the Islamic movement in the light of international change and the crisis in the Gulf]. Supervised by Ahmed Yousef. Produced and published in cooperation with USAR, Illinois.

ENGLISH

Proceedings of the Lunar Calendar Conference. Papers presented at the Conference of the Lunar Calendar. Edited by Dr 'Imad ad-Deen Ahmad (1408/1988).

The Education Conference Book. Edited by Dr. Fathi H. Malkawi and Dr. Hussein Abdul-Fattah. (1412/1991).

Islam and the Economic Challenge by Dr. M. Umer Chapra. (1412/1992). Published jointly with the Islamic Foundation.

JOURNALS

The American Journal of Islamic Social Sciences, Jointly published by the Institute and the Association of Muslim Social Scientists.

The Muslim World Book Review and its Supplement *Index of Islamic Literature*, Jointly published by the Institute and The Islamic Foundation.

AUDIO LIBRARY

ENGLISH

Islamization of Knowledge: General Principles, (IIIT) (forthcoming)

Outlines of a Cultural Strategy by Dr Ṭāhā J. al 'Alwānī. Read by Gai Eaton.

Islamization of Knowledge: A Methodology by Dr 'Imad al Din Khalil. Read by Gai Eaton.

Toward a Proper Reading of the Sunnah by Dr Ṭāhā J. al 'Alwānī. Read by Gai Eaton.

The Qur'an: The Primary Source of Knowledge by Dr Ṭāhā J. al 'Alwānī. Read by Gai Eaton.

The Qur'an and Modern Science by Dr Imad al Din Khalil. Read by H. Ashdown.

Toward a Global Cultural Renewal by Dr Muna AbulFadl. Read by Sam Dastor.

Ijtihad by Dr Ṭāhā J. al 'Alwānī. Read by H. Ashdown.

Islamization: Reforming Contemporary Knowledge by Dr. AbdulHamīd AbūSulaymān. Read by Sam Dastor.

Laxity, Moderation and Extremism in Islam by Aisha B. Lemu. Read by Gai Eaton.

ARABIC
Al Azma al Fikriyah al Mu'asirah [The Contemporary Intellectual Crisis] by Dr Ṭāhā J. al 'Alwānī. Read by Hasan Abu Alala.

Qadiyat al Manhajiyyah fi Fikr al Islami [The Issue of Methodology in Islamic Thought] by Dr. AbdulHamīd AbūSulaymān. Read by Hasan Abu Alala.

Al Bu'd al Gha'ib fi Fikr wa Mumarasat al Harakat al Diniyah [The Missing Dimension in Religious Movements] by Dr. Tāhā J. al Alwānī. Read by Dr. Bassam Saeh.

Al Jam' Bayna al Qirā'atain: Qira'at al Wahī wa Qira'at al Wujūd [Towards Understanding Revelation and Reality] by Dr. Ṭāhā J. al 'Alwānī. Read by Dr Bassam Saeh.

DISTRIBUTORS OF IIIT PUBLICATIONS

Belgium: Secompex, Bd. Mourice Lemonnier, 152, 1000 Bruxelles Tel: (32-2) 512-4473 Fax: (32-2) 512-8710

Egypt: IIIT Office, 26-B Al Jazirah al Wusta St., Zamalek, Cairo Tel: (202) 340-9520 Fax: (202) 340-9520

France: Libraire Essalam, 135 Boulevard de Ménilmontant 75011 Paris Tel: (33-1) 4338-1956 Fax: (33-1) 4357-4431

Holland: Rachad Export, Le Van Swindenstr. 108 II, 1093 Ck. Amsterdon Tel: (31-20) 693-3735 Fax: (31-20) 693-882x

India: Genuine Publications & Media (Pvt.) Ltd., P.O. Box 9725, Jamia Nagar, New Delhi 110 025 Tel: (91-11) 630-989 Fax: (91-11) 684-1104

Jordan: IIIT Office, P.O. Box 9489, Amman Tel: (962-6) 639-992 Fax: (962-2) 611-420

Lebanon: IIIT, c/o United Arab Bureau, P.O. Box 135788, Beirut Tel: (961-1) 807-779 Fax: c/o (212) 478-1491

Morocco: Dār al Amān for Publishing and Distribution, 4 Zangat al Ma'muniyah, Rabat Tel: (212-7) 723-276 Fax: (212-7) 723-276

Saudi Arabia: International House for Islamic Books, P.O. Box 55195, Riyadh 11534 Tel: (966-1) 465-0818 Fax: (966-1) 463-3489

United Arab Emirates: Reading for All Bookshop, P.O. Box 11032, Dubai Tel: (971-4) 663-903 Fax: (971-4) 690-084

United Kingdom: • Muslim Information Services, 233 Seven Sisters Road, London N4 2DA Tel: (44-71) 272-5170 Fax: (44-71) 272-3214
• The Islamic Foundation, Markfield Da'wah Centre, Ratby Lane, Markfield, Leicester LE6 ORN Tel: (44-530) 244-944/45 Fax: (44-530) 244-946

U.S.A.: • Islamic Book Service, 10900 W. Washington St., Indianapolis, IN 46231 Tel: (317) 839-9248 Fax: (317) 839-2511
• Al Sa'dāwi/United Arab Bureau, P.O. Box 4059, Alexandria, VA 22303 Tel: (703) 329-6333 Fax: (703) 329-8052

To order IIIT Publications write to the above listed distributors or contact: IIIT Department of Publications, P.O. Box 669 Herndon, VA 22070-4705 Tel: (703) 471-1133 Fax: (703) 471-3922